Simply Science

ELECTRICITY

Discover Science Through Facts and Fun

By Felicia Law

Science and curriculum consultant:

Debra Voege, M.A., science curriculum resource teacher

Gareth Stevens
Publishing

Please visit our web site at www.garethstevens.com.
For a free catalog describing our list of high-quality books, call 1-800-542-2595 (USA)
or 1-800-387-3178 (Canada). Our fax: 1-877-542-2596

Library of Congress Cataloging-in-Publication Data
Law, Felicia.
      Electricity/by Felicia Law
          p. cm.—(Simply Science)
      Includes bibliographical references and index.
      ISBN-10: 1-4339-0031-9   ISBN-13: 978-1-4339-0031-0 (lib. bdg.)
      1. Electricity—Juvenile literature. 2. Electric power—Juvenile literature. I. Title.
  QC527.2.L39   2009
  537—dc22   2008027572

This North American edition first published in 2009 by
Gareth Stevens Publishing
A Weekly Reader® Company
1 Reader's Digest Road
Pleasantville, NY 10570-7000 USA

This edition copyright © 2009 by Gareth Stevens, Inc. Original edition copyright © 2007 by
Diverta Publishing Ltd., First published in Great Britain by Diverta Publishing Ltd., London, UK.

Gareth Stevens Executive Managing Editor: Lisa M. Herrington
Gareth Stevens Creative Director: Lisa Donovan
Gareth Stevens Designer: Keith Plechaty
Gareth Stevens Associate Editor: Amanda Hudson
Gareth Stevens Publisher: Keith Garton
Special thanks to Jessica Cohn

Photo Credits: Cover (tc) Yanta/Shutterstock Inc., (bl) Kondrachov Vladimir/Shutterstock Inc.; pp. 4–5 Iksung Nah/Alamy; p. 6 Andre Seale/Alamy; p. 7 Jhaz Photography/Shutterstock Inc.; p. 8 Eugene Comstock/Shutterstock Inc.; p. 9 Art Directors; p. 10 Pchemyan Georgiy/Shutterstock Inc.; p. 11 (tl) Walter Matheson/Shutterstock Inc., (tr) Thomas Mounsey/Shutterstock Inc.; p. 12 PHOTOTAKE Inc./Alamy; p. 13 Jeremy Walker/SCIENCE PHOTO LIBRARY; p. 14 (b) N.A., Switzerland/Shutterstock Inc.; pp. 14–15 Vario Images GmbH & Co.KG/Alamy; p. 16 Peter Bowater/Alamy; p. 17 Lester Lefkowitz/ CORBIS; p. 18 (bc) Michele Otri/Shutterstock Inc., (r) Kondrachov Vladimir/Shutterstock Inc.; p. 21 Harald Høiland Tjøstheim/Shutterstock Inc.; p. 22 Tomasz Trojanowski/Shutterstock Inc.; p. 23 (tl) David Andrew Gilder/Shutterstock Inc., (cr) Yanta/Shutterstock Inc., (bl) Feng Yu/Shutterstock Inc., (br) 4uphoto.pt/Shutterstock Inc.; p. 25 Polina Lobanova/Shutterstock Inc.; p. 28 (tr) Chinch Gryniewicz/ CORBIS, (cr) William Casey/Shutterstock Inc.; p. 29 (t) Robert Francis/CORBIS, (br) Debra Weatherley.

Illustrations: Steve Boulter and Xact Studio

Diagrams: Karen Radford

Every effort has been made to trace the copyright holders for the photos used in this book, and the publisher apologizes in advance for any unintentional omissions. We would be pleased to insert the appropriate acknowledgements in any subsequent edition of this publication.

Printed in the United States of America

1 2 3 4 5 6 7 8 9 13 12 11 10 09

CONTENTS

What Is Electricity?

You can see what electricity does. It makes lights come on and runs appliances. In your home, electricity runs through wires. When you flick a switch on the wall, the power is there. But did you know that electricity is in the air and the ground? It's in every object around—it's even in YOU!

Electricity is everywhere!

   It helps light things up …

heat things …

   send messages …

power vehicles …

   and make machines work.

Electricity lights up this merry-go-round and makes it spin.

Electricity All Around

If you've ever seen a thunderstorm, you've probably seen a flash of lightning streak across the sky. Lightning is a great spark of electricity in the air.

Your body is full of electricity, too, although it's not as powerful as that lightning bolt. Your heart makes tiny amounts of electricity, which help it to beat properly. Your brain uses electricity to send messages all over your body through nerves.

Electric Eels

Electric eels produce electricity in their bodies like all animals do. The electric eel uses electricity as a weapon, though. This fish is found in the Amazon and Orinoco rivers in South America. It uses its electric power to stun its prey and shock its enemies to drive them away. In fact, it can produce enough electricity to light 12 light bulbs!

When lightning looks like this, it is called forked lightning.

Lightning

Lightning is a powerful electric spark. This spark is so strong that it can set trees and houses on fire or even burn the ground. It can kill a person with the force of its shock.

A lightning conductor is a thick wire on a building. Its job is to carry lightning away from the building and prevent damage. One end is fixed to the top of the building. The other is buried in the ground.

Moving Electrons

Electricity is found everywhere! Everything contains tiny, invisible particles of electricity called electrons.

Electrons zip around and around. In some kinds of materials, electrons can be pushed along, moving other electrons with them and creating a stream of electrons. This moving stream is an **electric current**.

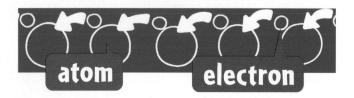

One electron has only a tiny bit of energy and moves just a short distance when pushed. A simple **battery**, however, can start up millions of electrons.

Conductors

Electrons move easily through materials known as conductors. One of the best conductors is the metal copper. This is why many of the electric wires used in your house are made from copper.

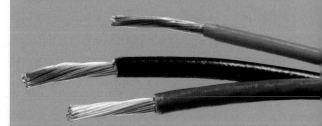

Insulators

Electrons do not move through materials called insulators. Plastic is an insulator. That is why copper wires are covered with plastic. It helps control the electrical current and keeps people safe.

Atoms

An electron is a tiny speck of matter. It is one of the parts of an **atom**. Everything in the world is made of atoms. All atoms have one or more electrons spinning around their center, called the nucleus.

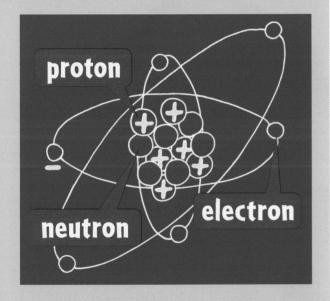

There are three parts to an atom. The **neutrons** are at the nucleus. They give off no **charge**.

The **protons** are also in the nucleus of the atom. They have a positive charge.

The **electrons** zip around the nucleus in wide orbits. They have a negative charge.

Static Electricity

Static electricity is a kind of energy that builds up when electrons move from one object to another. One object gets the electrons. The other loses them. If you use a plastic comb on a dry day, you can feel static electricity at work. Your hair may even crackle. If you feel a tiny shock when you touch something metal, like a door knob, that is usually static electricity that has built up.

Amps and Volts

When wires join a battery to a light bulb, the battery pushes electrons around the wires. The electrons go through the bulb, making it glow. The strength of this push is measured in volts. The more volts, the stronger the push.

V for Volt!

The volt, or V for short, is a unit of measurement. **Voltage** is measured with a voltmeter. The volts supplied to a house are between 110 and 230 volts.

The word volt comes from the name of the man who invented the first battery—an Italian man named Alessandro Volta. He placed the metals copper and zinc in salt water. Their electrons started moving. The salt water began to react with the metals, which caused electrical energy to be given off.

Batteries

A modern battery is made up of layers of chemicals inside a metal can. When the battery starts working, some of the chemicals break away and start eating at the metal container. The change to the can creates an electric current that flows out of the battery.

A for Amp!

The ampere, or A for short, is the unit for measuring an electric current. Amperes are often called amps. A current of about half an amp lights up an ordinary electric light bulb. In 1 amp, billions and billions of electrons flow every second!

An ammeter is an instrument used to measure the strength of an electric current in amperes.

The word amp comes from the name of the French scientist who invented a way of measuring an electric current, André-Marie Ampère.

Ampère was a brilliant mathematician. Together with other scientists, he showed how an electric current produces a magnetic field.

More importantly, he helped show how a powerful magnetic force can be created by electricity. This force is called **electromagnetism**.

Electromagnetism

An electromagnet has a special coil of wire wound around an iron rod. The rod works like a magnet. When electric current is switched on, it flows through the wire. If the current is off, the electromagnet loses its magnetism.

How a Magnet Works

A magnet is an object made of a kind of material, such as iron, which attracts objects like it. Magnets are surrounded by a pulling force known as a magnetic field. The field helps the magnet pull some metals toward it and push other ones away.

Generators and Motors

If a magnet spins in a coil of wire, its magnetic field makes electricity flow in the wires.

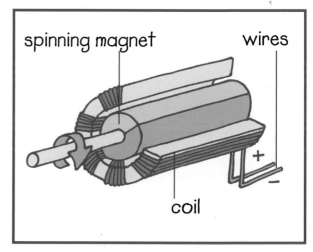

spinning magnet   wires

coil

A big magnet in a big coil generates a powerful flow. This is how electricity is generated in power stations. As the current flows in the coil, it makes the magnet spin, because its poles are attracted to the electric charge in the wires. The rod, attached to the magnet, also spins, which can turn a wheel or fan. That is how an electric motor runs!

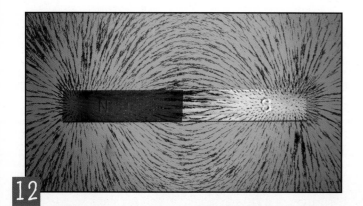

An Electromagnet in Action

electromagnet

scrap metal

Huge electromagnets are used in junkyards to help lift and move great chunks of metal from place to place.

1. The electromagnet hangs from the hook of a large crane. It is lowered toward the chunk of scrap metal.

2. The electric current is switched on. Then the electromagnet acts like a strong magnet, attracting the scrap metal.

3. The crane lifts its load of scrap and moves it to another place.

4. The electric current is switched off. The *magnet* loses its power to attract and the scrap drops to the ground.

Moved by Electricity

Electricity can be supplied to an electric motor by a battery or by a connection to an electricity supply.

Vehicles need to be able to move without being fixed to an electrical **circuit**. Trams and bumper cars use an aerial. That is an arm that rubs against wires, which power the vehicles.

The aerial on the roof of this tram gets power from overhead wires.

Moving Currents

An alternating current (AC) is an electric current that grows stronger, then weaker, and then changes direction. This happens over and over many times each second. This type of current is produced by generators, so it's the type of current that's supplied to your home.

A direct current (DC) is another kind of electric current. It flows through wires in one direction only. This kind of current flows from batteries.

At the Power Station

Most of the electricity we use in our homes is made in huge power stations.

Inside a power station, great wheels called **turbines** are turned by the force of hot steam. The wheels are made with curved blades. As they spin, they turn a pole attached to a generator. The generator makes electrical energy, and the **transformer** changes the electricity to the correct voltage to send to users.

Super-hot steam hits the blades of this turbine, making it spin.

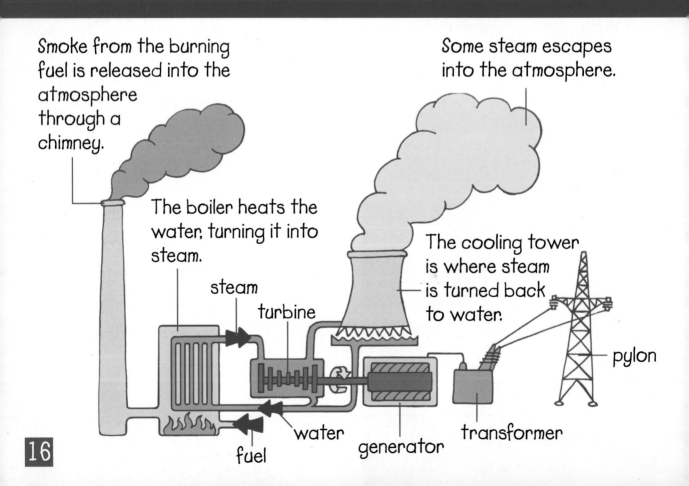

Smoke from the burning fuel is released into the atmosphere through a chimney.

Some steam escapes into the atmosphere.

The boiler heats the water, turning it into steam.

The cooling tower is where steam is turned back to water.

steam

turbine

pylon

water

fuel

generator

transformer

Hydro-Electric Power

Some power stations don't use steam to turn the turbines. They use fast-flowing water as it drops through pipes from the top of reservoirs. The water pushes the turbine blades as it rushes past, making electricity.

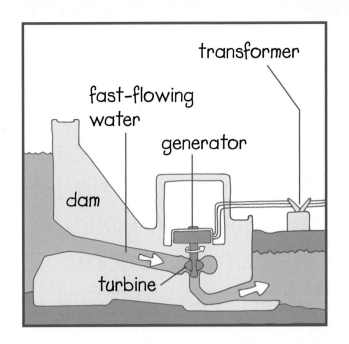

The Hoover Dam in Colorado is 725 feet (221 meters) high and 1,243 feet (379 m) wide! Hoover Dam forms Lake Mead, the largest U.S. lake made by humans.

Power to Your Home

Once the electricity has been generated at the power station, it must be carried to your home. It is brought there through a system of underground and overground cables. This system is known as a power grid.

Electricity is carried from power stations to towns and cities. It is sometimes carried across the countryside along huge overhead cables. The cables are held up by towers known as pylons.

cable

glass insulate

A pylon is a tower which is made from steel or wood. The cables hang from glass insulators fixed to the pylons. The insulators stop current from going down the pole and hurting living things.

Electricity Supply Grid

The power leaves the power station at a very high voltage, or power level. It travels across country on pylons at high voltage, too.

The power station can use coal, oil, gas, or nuclear energy as a fuel.

The high voltage power flows to special stations, containing transformers, where it is reduced so that factories, homes, schools, and offices can use it.

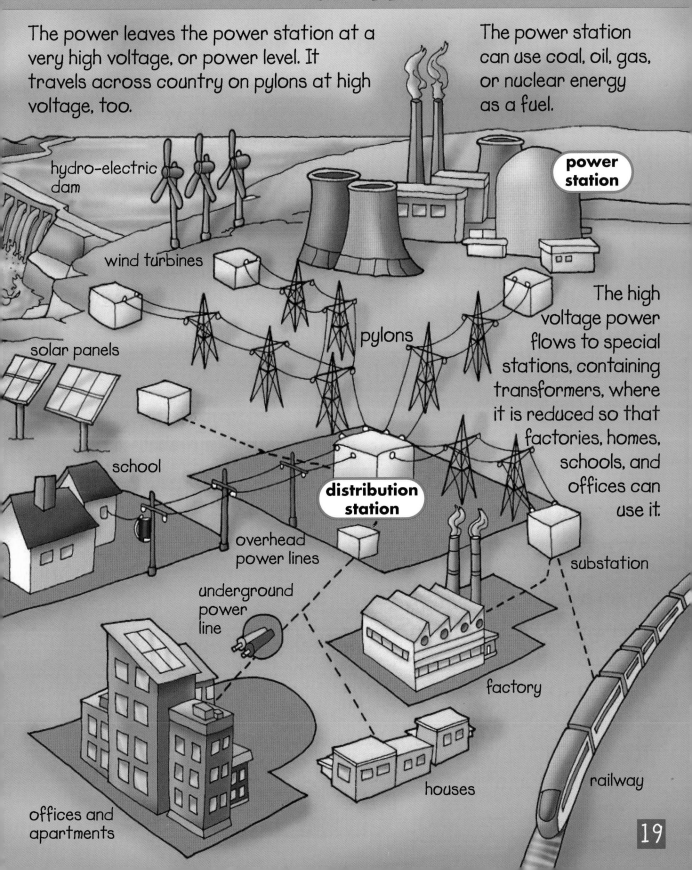

hydro-electric dam

wind turbines

solar panels

pylons

power station

school

distribution station

overhead power lines

underground power line

substation

factory

houses

railway

offices and apartments

Making It Safe

Electricity is useful, but it can be dangerous, too. Electricity enters your home through a large cable. Wiring in the walls, floors, and ceilings connects the power supply to the switches and plugs around the home. You use the plugs and switches to light up rooms, turn on televisions, or start computers.

When electricians install wiring in your home, they use special connections and circuits to make sure the electricity will turn on safely. You still need

Beware, Short Circuit!

If the plastic covering the wires wears off, the wires may touch. The current can then flow from one wire into the other. This is called a short circuit, and it's dangerous! The wires can overheat, which can cause a fire.

NEVER throw water on a fire caused by an electrical fault. Water conducts electricity!

WARNING

NEVER play with electric sockets or wires or touch them with wet hands. An electric shock could kill you!

Switching Off

Fuse

A fuse is a thin wire in an electric circuit. If there is too much current, the fuse becomes hot and melts. This switches off the electricity.

Circuit Breaker

A circuit breaker is an electric switch. It is connected to an electric circuit, and it cuts off the flow if too much current suddenly goes through the circuit.

Earth Wire

An earth wire is inside most electric cables in a house. It is also found in the cables that lead from an electric appliance. If there is an electrical **fault**, the earth wire leads the electric current safely away.

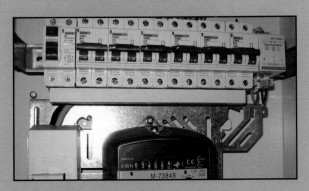

The different fuses in a fuse box (above) take care of different parts of a building.

A switch is a way of turning an electric current on . . .

. . . or off.

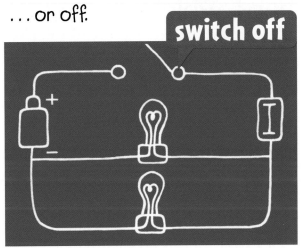

Inside the Wire

A typical electric cable has three wires. The live, or hot, wire carries current from the fuse box. A U.S. live wire is black, red, or blue. A white wire carries power back to the fuse box, which completes the circuit. The earth wire, which is green or bare, helps keep the flow safe.

Heating Up

As electrons push through thin wire, they give off energy in the form of heat. The electrons bump into each other and the atoms in the wire. The wire gives off heat, which we can use!

Electrical irons, kettles, toasters, and dryers all heat up in the same way. If you switch them on, an electric current passes along thin wire. The wire is made of a material, usually tungsten, that conducts the current easily, heating up as it does.

toaster

hairdryer

kettle

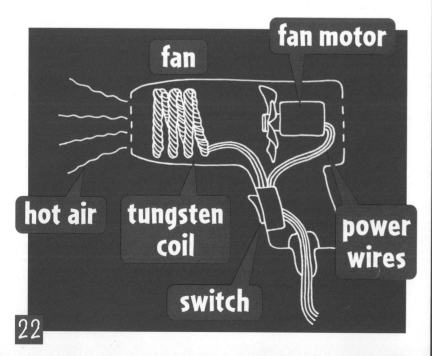

fan motor

fan

hot air

tungsten coil

switch

power wires

Heating Appliances

washing machine

iron

burner

A Kilowatt

A kilowatt is a unit of measurement that measures the power given off by an electric gadget. One kilowatt is 1,000 **watts**.

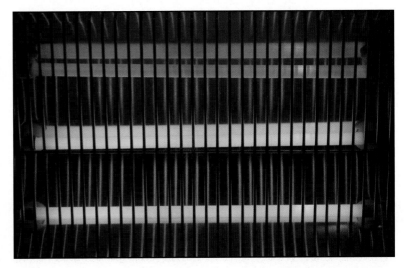

This furnace has a power of 3 kilowatts.

Tungsten

Tungsten is very hard metal. It is used in the heating coils inside many electrical gadgets, especially those that heat to high temperatures. Of all metals, tungsten has the highest melting point and highest strength at temperatures above 3002°F (1650 °C). When steel is mixed with tungsten, it becomes even tougher!

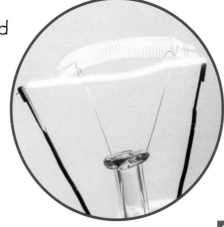

Switching on the Light

Thomas Alva Edison, an American inventor, grew up in a world where homes were lit by gas lamps and candles. You couldn't light up a house with the flick of a switch— not in those days!

A Bright Idea

1. Thomas Edison was a bright young man who moved from the Midwest to New Jersey. He went to work in a lab, creating inventions that would change people's lives.

2. Edison was deaf, so he invented devices to help deaf people. He also improved telegraph machines. In fact, he thought up over 1,000 inventions in his lifetime.

Low-Energy Light Bulbs

Low-energy light bulbs use only about $\frac{1}{5}$ the power of standard light bulbs but can last around 15 times longer, so they save a lot of energy. The bulbs are coated on the inside with a chemical called **phosphor**. A burst of energy when they're switched on excites gas inside them and makes the phosphor glow.

3. He is best known for making the first light bulb that was successful commercially. He developed a glass bulb that wouldn't melt when the glowing electric wire inside heated up. The secret was taking out all the air trapped inside the glass. That created a vacuum.

4. The electric current was passed through a tiny string of carbon which made it glow. A switch could stop and start the current flow.

Gadget Power

Modern homes need electricity for lighting, heating, cooking, and washing—and to power the gadgets used for information and entertainment. We use so much electricity, we need to start saving some!

Easy Swaps

Electric can opener Use muscle power on a hand-operated one.

Iron Wear clothes that don't crease, or hang them up.

Hairdryer Shake and towel-dry your hair instead. It's better for your hair anyway!

Oh, dear! The electricity supply has been cut, and there's no more power. It's time to remember how people managed before the days of electricity!

It's time to chop wood and light a fire for heat. Or you can use an old-fashioned heater that burns oil.

Food rotting in the refrigerator? Time to think about buying fresh food and eating it that day.

The lights have gone out. It's time to find some candles. Be careful with the flames!

When the heat shuts down, it's time to put on extra thick socks.

Time to wind up an older clock. It will need resetting as the spring inside winds down. With no alarm, you'll have to rely on the Sun, as your ancestors did!

The computer is down! You won't be able to go online after finishing your homework.

No television! What did your grandparents do? They read books, put on puppet shows, played games, and had fun together.

Bring Out the Batteries

If your power supply is off, you can still use gadgets that run on the stored electricity in batteries.

Electricity in the Future

We take electricity for granted, but a few hundred years ago, people lived without it. They did fine—mostly! The people burned wood for heat and cooking. They used the power of wind and water to drive their machines. They lit wax candles to light their homes at night.

Today, scientists are warning us that we must return to some of the old ways. Not only are our fuel supplies running out, but many fuels are doing a great deal of damage to our planet.

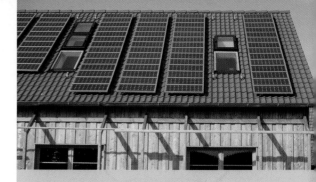

Solar Power

Solar panels can be used for changing sunlight energy to electricity. They are really useful in remote places—such as orbiting satellites!

Wind Power

Wind farms have tall poles with turbine blades turned by the force of the wind. Large wind farms provide power for national electrical grids, while a smaller turbine can power a building.

This is a geothermal power station in Wairakei, New Zealand. It produces more than 4 percent of the country's electricity!

Clockwork Power

This "clockwork" radio has a small generator inside it. When it's wound up. it produces enough electricity to power the radio for about 30 minutes!

Geothermal Power

This power comes from energy trapped in Earth's rocks. Geothermal energy can rush to Earth's surface as steam. The force of the steam can be used to drive turbines and make electricity. Hot water below the ground can be pumped to the surface and piped to homes to be used for heating.

Electricity Quiz

1. What are the tiny parts of atoms that carry electricity?

2. Who invented the world's first battery?

3. What feature of electricity is measured in amps or amperes?

4. What happens to an electromagnet when you switch it on?

5. Which part of your body uses electricity to send messages?

6. What part of a power station makes the magnets in the generator spin?

7. What type of electricity can be made at a dam?

8. What happens when a fuse melts?

9. Which metal has the highest melting point?

10. What important electrical device did Thomas Alva Edison develop?

1. Electrons 2. Alessandro Volta 3. The current 4. It becomes magnetic! 5. Your brain 6. The turbine 7. Hydroelectric 8. The current is switched off 9. Tungsten 10. The first commercial light bulb

Glossary

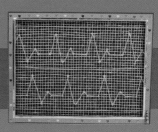

atom: the basic component of matter, made of an arrangement of tiny electrical particles called electrons (-), neutrons, and protons (+)

battery: a device that stores electricity

charge: a characteristic of individual electrical particles and groupings of the particles; adding electrons (-) can result in a negative charge; subtracting electrons can create a positive charge

circuit: the path over which an electrical current flows

distribution station: a place in a power grid that sends power to its substations, which direct power to smaller parts of the grid

electric current: a moving stream of electrons

electromagnetism: a pull from an electric current and a magnetic field

fault: a defect in an electrical wire or a circuit connection

generator: a machine that changes mechanical energy into electrical energy

phosphor: a chemical that glows in low-energy light bulbs

poles: the positive and negative points on a magnet or terminals on a battery

transformer: a device that changes electrical energy into a useful form

turbine: motors or engines with curved vanes around drive shafts; the vanes get turned by steam or another force and turn the shafts

voltage: a measure of the force in electricity

watts: basic units of power

Index